The Book of Travel Tips

Travel Safe, Travel Smart

Tessa Ingel

The Book of Travel Tips

Travel Safe, Travel Smart

Vanguard Press

A CIP catalogue record for this title is
available from the British Library.

ISBN 978 1 80016 791 9

*Vanguard Press is an imprint of
Pegasus Elliot Mackenzie Publishers Ltd.*
www.pegasuspublishers.com

First Published in 2024

**Vanguard Press
Sheraton House Castle Park
Cambridge England**

Printed & Bound in Great Britain

Dedication

This book is dedicated to my father, who inspired me to follow in his footsteps and explore the world.

"A mind stretched by new experiences can never go back to its old dimensions."
(Oliver Wendell-Holmes Jr.)

Dear fellow traveler,

Whether you prefer prepackaged tours, customized small group tours, independent travel, or backpacking, you'll find a host of helpful ideas in *Sights Uncovered Travel Tips*, which I have collected over many years from my personal experiences as well as from fellow travelers.

From step-by-step tips on planning your trip to choosing a wardrobe, finding drivers and guides, stretching travel dollars, dealing with lost luggage, staying safe and healthy, coping with jet lag, tipping, doing your laundry on the go, and much more.

Whether a first-time traveler or a seasoned adventurer, I hope that this book of useful tips will become your indispensable travel companion.

If you have any tips that you'd like to share, I'd love to hear from you, and if appropriate, post them on my travel website.

Please email me at travelwitht@sightsuncovered.com, and we'll let you know if we decide to use them. Wishing you safe, happy, and stress-free travels.

Bon voyage!

Tessa

Contents

ABOUT THE AUTHOR

I was born in South Africa, surrounded by multiple languages: English, Sotho, Zulu, Afrikaans, Russian, Portuguese, Greek, and Polish. Mozambique — which lies on the northeastern border of South Africa — was an exotic blend of Portugal and Africa. It was there, at around the age of six, that I was treated to my first taste of Portuguese — a musical language that to me sounded like water skipping over pebbles.

My parents were avid, adventurous, independent travelers. Every year, when manufacturing closed from December to mid-January, they would take off to explore the world. Our devoted grandparents would move in, and we would all wait impatiently for the postcards to arrive.

At the age of nine, I experienced the magic of Europe and the seeds of love for travel that were to bloom and nourish me for a lifetime were sown. My mom, dad, older sister, and I traveled to five countries. While our parents ventured to Russia and Poland, my sister and I spent three weeks with relatives in Paris.

Years later, after I graduated from high school in South Africa, I spent a year studying languages in Montreux — Switzerland. My school friends came from over twenty countries. It was akin to living in a mini-United Nations. When the school year ended, I spent the summer with my Greek friend, Mariana, in the Greek islands where her grandparents lived. I celebrated my 18th birthday on the island of Lesvos.

Back in South Africa, I attended university in Johannesburg, graduating with a four-year bachelor of arts degree in foreign languages and art history. My husband and I were married in South Africa and immigrated with two young children to the USA.

My first career in California was as an independent travel agent affiliated with an agency that did a large travel volume of tours to Mexico, a country that to this day, is one of the best-kept secrets.

Throughout my twenty-seven-year highly successful and rewarding career in financial services and insurance, we always made time to travel. Over the past ten years the length of our trips has increased to include multiple destinations. Thus far, we have visited seventy-two countries and continue to relish exploring new places and returning to those destinations that have a special allure.

We are always on the lookout for travel tips that make things go more smoothly and help us to get the most pleasure out of our travels. Here's to hoping that you uncover some helpful tips and put them to good use.

How to Plan Your own Trip

(Helpful Hints that Apply to all Travelers)

You can choose a package tour from ultraluxury to budget and everything in between; pay a travel agent to customize your trip, or plan your own journey and have total freedom. It may seem daunting, but when you develop a process, you'll soon find out how much you've been missing by turning over the planning phase to someone else. People ask me: "But how do you do it?" Here is a road map to guide you.

Planning our trips myself allows us to travel at our own pace; see the sites that interest us the most; have lots of free time to explore off-the-beaten-paths, nooks, and crannies; eat at hole-in-the-wall restaurants when they call to us; shop when the mood takes us or not shop at all; and not waste precious time waiting for members of the group who have gone astray or overslept.

Having said that, if you don't enjoy the planning process or don't have the time to plan your trip, choose a tour company that meets your needs. Ask questions such as: 'What is the maximum number of people in the group'?

'How much free time is there'? Ask to see different itineraries and study them carefully. Make sure that you know what is *not* included in the tour price. Are there options to add additional sites?

Although we travel solo, I use local tour companies when our itinerary calls for it and local drivers/guides.

Whether you decide to plan your own trip or choose a prepackaged tour, read: 'How *to Plan Your own Trip.* You'll find helpful hints that apply to all travelers.

1. Choose your destination.

2a. Research the weather. Weather can either make or spoil a trip. Examples of the latter: hiking the Inca Trail in Peru in the rainy season; visiting India during the monsoon season; going on Safari in Africa during the hot summer months; visiting Patagonia in November when the winds are at their most fierce or the Sahara in the most humid month of July or the windiest months of June, July, and August.

2b. weatherspark.com is an excellent site that will give you detailed weather information.

3a. Research the dates of festivals and major holidays taking place in the destination you plan to visit. Example: you may want to be in a particular place specifically because you'd like to witness and participate in a celebration. Bear in mind that locals are on the move during these times. Transport and accommodation are in greater demand so book early and expect to pay higher prices. Conversely — if you have no interest in witnessing the festivities, plan your itinerary to avoid the crowds and save money on your accommodation, guides, and transport.

3b. Research high season, low season, and the best season: those windows of time when the weather is mild, and the crowds have thinned in late autumn/early winter and early spring.

4. If budget is a concern, check your planned destination's exchange rate against your currency. If your money goes further, it can make a big difference in how much you can see and do.

5. Visas. Check visa requirements online.

Visas for some countries can take several weeks to secure. You can use a company that specializes in obtaining foreign visas to expedite the process. They stay on top of the ever-changing rules; know how the forms need to be completed; what documents, photos, itineraries, etcetera must accompany the visa application. While you have to pay for their services, they get the job done, and it's hassle-free. When visiting countries such as Russia and China, which have convoluted complex visitor requirements, I would highly recommend a company specializing in obtaining visas.

Some visas can be purchased online, some upon arrival at the airport before entering the country, but the long lines can be frustrating, eat up valuable time, and delay your fellow travelers.

Note: Euro Visas.

The ETIAS VISA– Since 2021 there has been talk of introducing the ETIAS VISA. It is now said that it will be implemented in 2025. US Citizens traveling to Europe will need to obtain the ETIAS visa to enter the 30 countries of the Schengen. The Schengen is made up of countries without internal borders where people move freely between nations. (I suggest that one go online closer to the time, and read up which documents and information the Schengen border officials may require you to produce.)

6. Decide how many days/weeks/months you can take for your upcoming trip.

7. Remember that travel days can be completely lost days, so schedule your flights, train rides, tours, etcetera, accordingly. To save time and accommodation costs, travel at night when feasible.

8. Check on health requirements and vaccinations. Make sure you have a copy of your immunizations with you, as you may very well be required to present proof to enter a country. Remember to check each country's website for immunization requirements.

9. If your flight makes a stop on the way to your destination, you may be able to stay there for a week or so at no additional or minimal cost. Don't overlook this. We have visited numerous destinations at no extra cost. Examples: Ireland, Dubai, Hong Kong, Japan, Spain, Holland, England, Switzerland, and many others. Check with the airline and compare airline stopovers.

10. Want to travel for free? Pay most of your living and business expenses using a credit card that allows you to accumulate air miles for every dollar spent. If the credit card is issued by a specific airline, for example, American

Airlines, United, Jet Blue, etcetera, check the airlines with which it partners. Alternatively, choose a credit card that allows you to redeem your air miles with any airline. Example: American Express or Capital One Venture Card. Also, choose a credit card that does not charge a foreign exchange fee every time you use the card outside your home country.

The Nitty Gritty of Putting Your Trip Together

Here you will find a list of resources. You'll get into the process of how to map out your trip and then fill in the important details. After reading and implementing these steps, you'll be almost ready to hit the road with confidence.

1. You have chosen your destination, read up on the 'must-see' highlights and those things of interest to you, which could be as simple as visiting a particular neighborhood in a city and having sufficient time to wander, people watch, and soak up the atmosphere. Resources: *Footprint, Frommer's, Fodor's, Lonely Planet, Rough Guides, Eyewitness Travel Guides, Insight Guides, National Geographic Travel Guides, Rick Steves' Europe,* visitacity.com, blogs and articles found on internet travel sites, travel magazines, and the weekend travel page of newspapers such as *The New York Times, The Los Angeles Times, The Wall Street Journal,* etcetera. The site www.roadtrippers.com can be helpful in planning a road trip. You put in your starting point and destination, and it will give you places of interest, accommodation, restaurants, homestays, etcetera, along your route.

I like to have a hard copy of a book and print information off the internet so that I can highlight, tab, and mark up pages, which helps me with my planning.

2a. Get a map of the area that you intend to visit so that you can plan the flow of your trip to avoid backtracking, which can be a time waster and add to the costs. Also, consult a world map to see what countries and islands are in the general area you'll be visiting. You may be able to arrange a stopover at a terrific destination at little or no extra cost to the purchase price of your airline ticket.

2b. I plan our trips with the most strenuous and active touring, hiking, etcetera at the beginning of the trip, chilling out and relaxing on a beach, a boat, or in the mountains at the end. I find relaxing the mind first, and then the body works best for us. Give some thought to the order that will work best for you.

3. Take a calendar and photocopy the pages of the days/weeks/months you plan to travel, or get a sheet of poster board and make your own calendar.

4. Using the information you have gleaned from points one and two above, fill in where you plan to spend each day and night. *Important:* research religious days of the week, public holidays, festivals, and museum closing days. We were in Catalonia — Spain on Dia de Reis, and there was not a living soul in sight except for those lined up outside the bakery to collect their festival cakes topped with a crown.

5. Decide how you will get from one country or city to another. Fly, train, boat, bus, rent a car or hire a driver.

6. Fill that in on your calendar: red pen — fly; blue pen — bus; yellow pen — train; green pen — drive; turquoise pen — boat.

7a. Research road conditions (essential if you plan on driving). Driving yourself in Italy is one thing — whereas driving in India is suicidal. Trains in Japan are the most efficient means of transport, whereas, in South Africa, they're virtually non-existent.

7b. Fill in the approximate time needed to travel from one destination to another on your calendar flowchart. It's as simple as Googling travel time from point A to point B. Allow extra time for delays and stops along the way. Remember: if you are driving, the journey *is* the destination, so you want to have enough time to stop and linger a while.

8a. Allow for 'buffer' time (sometimes an entire day) to recuperate from many hours of travel the previous day. Buffer days are perfect for getting to know a city, wandering and discovering on your own, sitting at a café and people watching, getting laundry done, etcetera.

8b. *Important:* Don't plan to go on a major tour the day you arrive at your destination or the following day. Flights, weather conditions, and strikes can mean that you could land up missing a tour for which you have prepaid a substantial amount.

9. Check on the time differences within the zones of countries you will be visiting, the time changes when you move from one country to another, and the time differences between your home country and destination.

Time changes can affect your planning. You may have a long flight and gain time, which gives you additional hours to explore your destination. Conversely, you may have a relatively short flight and lose time. Check the time changes when you are driving from one destination to another. You could cross into a different time zone and find all gas stations, restaurants, banks, stores, museums, etcetera closed.

10a. Whether one should book hotels ahead of time depends on individual preference. You may want to have the freedom to just go with the flow and travel without reservations. I generally book hotels ahead of time or at least decide on the neighborhood where we'd like to stay, which saves time and sometimes money. Remember that unique inns, boutique hotels, and the most charming B&Bs, often have limited accommodation and can fill up a year or more in advance. Conversely, last-minute bookings can result in superior accommodation at significantly reduced rates. Many hoteliers would prefer to get less revenue for an available suite than let it stand empty. You may have to do some polite bargaining and negotiating, but it's worth the effort if you succeed.

10b. Groups generally make block bookings several months in advance. Within approximately thirty days of their arrival date, they begin relinquishing unsold accommodation, so check in regularly, and you may very well snag a booking at the last minute.

10c. hotels.com; bookings.com; expedia.com; boutiquehotels.com; designhotels.com; airbnb.com;

tripadvisor.com — are all sites where one can research a host of accommodations from budget to five-star and make online bookings — trivago.com compares the rates offered by various sites and shows you which one has the best rates for any given property. One can also try the hotel's website. Check and compare rates.

10d. Don't forget the old-fashioned way: direct communication. Establish a rapport with the owner/manager by calling or emailing hotels, inns, and B&Bs directly. This is often my preferred method, even though it's a little more time-consuming. By doing this, we get the type of room we prefer: with a view; a balcony; quiet; on a higher floor; etcetera and we connect with local people who have terrific contacts for drivers, guides, local tour operators, museums, and restaurants.

10e. Fill in the name and contact information of your hotel on your calendar flow sheet.

11. Give some thought to which part of your trip you would like to do independently and where you may be better off taking a group tour; hiring a driver or a driver and guide. Many tours can be booked at the last minute. However, some tours must be booked well in advance if you don't want to be faced with disappointment. Examples: hiking the Inca Trail in Peru; traveling to remote parts of the Amazon; trekking to the hill tribes in Vietnam; African Safaris; hiking down the Grand Canyon and staying overnight, etcetera.

12a. I use local tour companies that have favorable reviews. For private day tours and drivers, I contact the hotel where we'll be staying and ask the manager/owner to arrange a reliable, safe driver and an English-speaking guide. We've never yet been disappointed. On the contrary, we've met some of our finest guides and drivers using this approach and have made some lifelong friends. If we have a particularly good cab ride and I can communicate reasonably well in a common language, I'll ask the cab driver if he'd like to be our driver for a few days. We've had some wonderful drivers in Ecuador, Peru, Bali, India, and Mexico.

12b. One of our excellent finds has been: toursbylocals.com. You can read the guide's bio, choose someone who appeals to you and communicate directly with the guide.

12c. Many cities have hop-on hop-off city tour buses, which can be a terrific and inexpensive introduction to a city. It's a way to get a peek at the highlights and neighborhoods and decide where you'd like to spend more time.

12d. https://mydaytrip.com provides excellent service across the globe. Local drivers will pick you up in one town/city and drive you to the next. You can request that they stop at places of interest along the way.

13. Arriving sleep-deprived in a foreign country, at a chaotic airport, where cab drivers and touts bombard you, and you don't speak the language, can be overwhelming and highly stressful. If your budget allows, I strongly suggest that you email your hotel before you arrive and ask them to send a driver/taxi to meet you. Tell them that the

driver must meet you as you exit baggage claim with a sign bearing your name in bold print. Ask them what the fee will be ahead of time so that there is no bargaining and haggling with the driver. This small step makes a world of difference to how you feel when you reach your destination. Remember: if your flight is delayed, email the hotel and let them know or you may be charged an additional fee to compensate the driver for his time. Better yet, make sure that you ask for the driver's email and cell phone number so that you can contact him/her directly in the event of a significant delay.

14. By creating this flow chart, I have a clear idea of how the trip will flow, what reservations need to be made, how we will get from one destination to another, whether I've budgeted enough time or too little time in one place, etcetera. Remember: "If you don't flow it, you don't know it".

15. Consider how much you want to pack into each day. Overscheduling your activities can lead to disappointment if you find that it is not possible to see and do all that you'd looked forward to doing, as well as fatigue and burnout.

16. When your planning is done, the final step is to draw up an itinerary to carry with you. You should also give a copy to your family or a trusted friend at home. I take a printed copy and have access to an electronic copy. Bear in mind that you may not always have access to the internet.

17. Specialized group theme tours.

If you have a particular interest, organized group theme tours can be a wonderful way to immerse yourself in your given interest or hobby and connect with others who share your passion. However, I would suggest that you read the itinerary carefully so as not to suffer from theme burnout. Whether it be scuba diving, bird watching, temples, antiquities, art history, etcetera, it can sometimes become overwhelming.

How to Find Better Fares

1. The time of year that you travel can make a difference to your ticket price. Generally, mid-January to the end of March is less expensive. The holidays are over, people are back to work, and children are back in school.

2. The day — weekend versus midweek — and time of day that you fly can make a difference. Booking a red-eye flight, early morning or mid-morning Tuesday or Wednesday flight, or a Saturday midday flight may be cheaper. Helpful sites for doing research: kayak.com and momondo.com.

3. Remember that even a non-refundable ticket is refundable within twenty-four hours of purchase. If you find a ticket that looks as though it might work for you, grab it and keep searching. Just don't forget to cancel the nonrefundable booking within twenty-four hours if you find something better.

4. Connecting flights, as opposed to direct flights, are often cheaper. See where the flight connects. You may be able to spend a few days in a cool destination that you hadn't considered. It's also pleasant to break a long journey, stretch your legs, take a nap, or freshen up. We've booked into hotels or pods at the connecting airport and

had a few hours of comfortable sleep, which makes a long journey more tolerable.

5. Check which airlines fly from your city of departure directly to their home country. Their rates may be more favorable.

6. Two one-way fares, instead of a roundtrip fare, can sometimes be a better deal, and a roundtrip ticket may be cheaper than a one-way. You simply don't use the return portion of the ticket.

7a. When booking the airline tickets for a trip that involves multiple flights, I find that purchasing the outbound flight and the return flight on one ticket with the same carrier generally works best. I then book the in-between flights separately — for example, Los Angeles, to South Africa, India to Los Angeles, as one ticket.

7b. When booking a multicity flight with the same carrier, check the prices of two separate tickets versus a multicity ticket. Example: On Aero Mexico's site, I recently researched a multicity flight: Mexico City to Villahermosa and Huatulco to Los Angeles. The price for two adult economy tickets was $2500. Two unlinked, separate tickets were $1,010, which included the fee for seat selection.

7c. Consider using different carriers if their schedules and fares work better for you. Remember: there's no reason to link your tickets.

8a. How far in advance should one book? If you book too early, you'll overpay; if you book too close to your departure date, you could overpay big time! For international, I generally book four to six months before departure, depending on the destination and whether we are planning a visit during the high or low season. I always recommend checking whether there are any upcoming public holidays, religious holidays, or festivals taking place in our chosen destinations. Any one of these may require you to book a year in advance, depending on how many visitors they traditionally attract.

8b. For domestic book three and a half months before if its high season — and around five to six weeks ahead for regular travel. Unfortunately, the best way is to keep checking in and monitor the fares to your desired destination and grab a good fare when you see it.

**Note:* If you use Hopper, Kayak, and Skyscanner sites, you may want to use them for researching flights and then book directly with the airline. When booking domestic flights within a foreign country, be aware of their high season, national, and religious holidays, when prices may spike or drop.

9. Traveling on the day of a public holiday may save you money, whereas flying on the days leading up to a public holiday or the days following a public holiday is likely to be more costly.

10. Alert! Pay careful attention when booking connecting flights. Give yourself adequate time to get through customs (if required), collect baggage (if need be), and get from your gate of arrival to your gate of departure, which can be a mile apart. *Do not* be misled by what an airline calls a 'legal' connecting time. Their connecting

times often have nothing to do with reality. You also have to consider that you are likely to miss your connecting flight if your first flight runs late. As for your checked luggage, chances are you're not going to be seeing it for a while.

Having experienced the stress of finding ourselves in this situation and having witnessed the stress that it causes fellow travelers, I now make sure that we don't fall into this trap.

Airline Reservations; Baggage; Credit Cards, U.S.D, and ATMs

1a. Airline reservations. When making reservations online, be careful of booking your ticket through an online travel company versus booking directly through the airline. Should you need to make any changes to your itinerary or wish to make upgrades such as seat selection, you'll be given the run around between the online agency and the airline.

1b. If you book the lowest economy fare online, be prepared to be squashed into the rear of the plane and be allocated the worst seat.

1c. Go online and check SeatGuru before choosing your seat. Select and pay for your seat online or call the airline.

1d. Some airlines will not allow you to select or even pay to select your seat if you fly economy class. In this case, go online twenty-four hours before your flight and reserve your seat.

2a. If the airline cancels your flight and moves you to an alternate flight or changes the flight time, you'll most likely receive an email from the online agency. Read it carefully! I cannot stress this strongly enough! We had the experience of the online agency accepting a change on our behalf without consulting us. The change would have resulted in our international flight from Dallas to Rome, boarding twenty minutes before our domestic flight from Los Angeles arrived in Dallas! When we tried to change it, we were told by the airline that since one change had already been made to the ticket — the online agency accepting the change on our behalf — we would have to pay for a second change. Getting this fixed was a nightmare that I don't wish on anyone.

2b. Be aware that when the airlines change their schedule or a flight, it's not uncommon for them to drop your seat allocation even if you've paid for it. So remember, check all communication from the airline or online agency, line by line. Don't take anything for granted.

3. Airline seating. It's common for airlines to partner (codeshare) with other airlines on international flights. Example: American Airlines with British Air, Qantas, Iberia, Cathay Pacific, etcetera United with South African Airlines, Air New Zealand, Lufthansa, etcetera. Make sure to call each carrier on your flight itinerary to book your seating. Don't assume that because you chose your seat when you booked online, the airline won't change it, especially if you paid a bargain fare.

4. Baggage allowance. Traveling with multiple carriers can present some challenges, especially on international trips, where you have domestic flights within a country. Each airline may have different baggage

allowance rules, so check online or call the airline. You may want to pay the additional baggage fee in advance and make sure that they email you proof of payment. If you wait to pay at the check-in counter, it causes delays and depending on the country, you could be charged whatever the person checking you in decides they feel like charging. It can be pretty random.

5. Tag your bags properly. Before handing your luggage to the check-in clerk, attach a luggage tag with your home address and a second tag on which you write your destination — the date — the address of your destination — your email address — and the email of the hotel where you would like to receive your luggage should it get lost.

6. Luggage tags can get lost or eaten by the conveyor belts, so take one extra precaution: stick your information to the inside of your bag — where it is clearly visible.

7. Use a colored strap and /or a piece of ribbon tied tightly to the handle of your suitcase to make it easier to identify at baggage claim and reduce the chances of someone else walking off with your luggage.

8. Take a photo of your luggage just before checking it with the airline. If it goes astray, you'll have to fill out a report. The more clearly you can describe your luggage, the better. Don't assume that all airports have sophisticated baggage tracking systems.

9. Avoid theft. Some airports and countries are notorious for going through your luggage. If the airport has a baggage wrap service where they wrap your checked

suitcase in plastic, use it. The wrapping makes it less likely that rummagers on a stealing spree will select your bag. Note: Some airport wrapping services offer wrapping plus strapping. My experience has been that the strapping is not necessary. On the contrary, if you have liquids in your luggage, they may leak, and fragile items may crack due to tight strapping.

10a. Carry U.S.D. I recommend always traveling with several hundred U. S. dollars. You never know where your travels may take you. Don't assume that things always go smoothly. Flights get redirected due to weather conditions; buses, cabs, and cars break down in remote places; ATMs run out of money. We experienced this in Iguazu, Argentina, when the ATMs had no cash for three days following a public holiday. U.S. dollars are welcome in most places, and sometimes you may even get significant discounts in stores and small hotels that are happy to be paid in cash, especially in U.S. dollars.

10b. In Asia, new, crisp, one-hundred-dollar bills can get you discounts. Order them from your bank a week or two before your departure.

11. Credit cards. Always take more than one credit card when traveling and don't carry them in the same wallet. If you are a couple traveling together, make sure that you have at least one credit card in each of your names. Five days into one of our two-and-a-half-month trips, my husband's ID was stolen. Fortunately, I was carrying two different cards in my name only.

12. ATMs. The safest places to obtain local currency are often the airport's arrival terminal or at an ATM inside a reputable bank. Even there, however, check that no one is standing close to you and run your hand over the machine where you insert your card, punch in your code, etcetera, to make sure that there are no parts attached to the machine that could be capturing your information.

13. Before completing your transaction, check the exchange fee. In some airports, towns, and cities, it can be exorbitant, particularly in high-volume tourist areas. Just cancel the transaction and find another ATM.

14. Notify your bank before embarking on your journey as to how long you'll be traveling and which countries you'll be visiting. Generally, the notification is only valid for ninety days. Remember to contact your bank before the ninety-day period expires if you'll be out of the USA for longer, to avoid your ATM withdrawals being declined.

Car Rental in Foreign Countries

1. Large cities can have multiple airports. Check the airport name and code and make sure that you reserve your car pick up and drop off at the correct airport.

2. Contact your hotel and ask where the closest car rental is unless, of course, you are renting at the airport. Cities and neighborhoods within cities can be bigger than one thinks, and you want to avoid the inconvenience of having to trek across the city to pick up or drop off a car.

3. Automatic versus stick shift. Be aware that there are countries where stick shift is still very popular. If you are not comfortable driving a stick shift car, make sure that you stipulate that you must have an automatic vehicle.

4. Most cars today come with GPS, or you can use an app on your cell phone such as Google Maps or Waze. Hint: if you have the time and want to see the countryside set your GPS to avoid freeways and highways. You will be treated to an enchanting journey of discovering the countryside, local villages, marketplaces, and meeting the local people. (Check on whether it's safe for a foreigner to drive through the villages and towns that you'll be passing through) .

5. Before leaving the car rental, take an extra few minutes to examine the car's interior and exterior and take photos with your cell phone of any scratches, dings, and dents. It's advisable to also take photos or a video of the interior and exterior of the vehicle when returning it to the car rental company. Travelers have reported having their credit cards charged several days or weeks after returning the car, for nonexistent damages.

6. Don't forget to pack your driver's license.

Verify what your credit card's auto insurance does and does not cover and purchase additional insurance if necessary. Make sure that you are adequately insured before driving off with your rental car.

7. Confirm that you are driving on the correct side of the road in the country where you are renting a car. U.S. China, Russia, most of Europe, and South America drive on the right side.

Japan, the United Kingdom, Ireland, Cyprus, Malta, Guyana, Suriname, Australia, New Zealand, India, South Africa, Kenya, Zimbabwe, Zambia, Namibia, Uganda, Tanzania, Hong Kong, Pakistan, Sri Lanka, Malaysia, Singapore, Indonesia, Bangladesh, and Thailand all drive on the left. Most countries that were once British colonies drive on the left. Check on a site such as worldatlas.com.

8. Quick tips to make sure that you are driving on the correct side of the road: as the driver, you should always be in the middle of the road — in other words, *not* next to the curb.

Example: If the passenger seat is on your left, you should be driving on the left side of the street.

9. A few countries require you to have an international driver's license in addition to your home country's state license. Visit your local AAA office or go to their website: aaa.com to apply for an international license and carry it with you at all times when driving in foreign countries.

10. If you are renting a car in Europe, check that your rental car is equipped with warning triangles, reflective vests, a first aid kit, and a blank European accident report form. You'll need these in case of an accident and may be fined if you can't produce them.

11. Google the road signs of the countries where you will be driving. You're likely to come across signs that you've never seen before. They can be hard to figure out, especially some of those in rural areas and historical old towns.

12. Many cities have "old towns" where parking is usually restricted to cars owned by locals who have special permits. Don't risk parking in these areas. The rule is often enforced with hidden cameras.

13. If you are driving with children, check whether they need to be sitting in booster seats in the back of the car. It's determined by their height, weight, and age, and may differ from the rules you are accustomed to in your home country.

14. In some countries, the traffic police issue "spot fines," which means that they have to be paid immediately

in cash. Make sure to always have cash on you when driving in a foreign country.

15. While giving a roadside bribe to a traffic cop is commonplace in some countries, be careful not to do this. It can land you in trouble.

16. Be aware that if you are over or under a certain age, you may not be permitted to rent a car in certain countries, and it may vary between regions within a country. Check this detail.

17. We always purchase a local newspaper and leave it on the back seat. Car thieves are more likely to think that you are a local versus a tourist and choose another car.

18. Be aware that in some countries, if you go through a yellow traffic light, you'll get a traffic violation ticket.

19. It's a good idea to carry a tire pressure gauge if you intend to rent a car. Most of them don't come with pressure gauges.

20. Don't forget to take a car cellphone charger. Using navigation systems such as Waze and Google Maps for several hours can use a lot of cellphone battery.

Parking and Navigating the Narrow Streets of Historic Towns

1. Most historical old towns in Eastern and Western Europe have limited accessibility for resident cars and virtually none for non-resident cars, which makes reaching your hotel an interesting and often frustrating challenge, especially if you don't speak the language and Google Maps and Waze announce: "You have reached your destination.!" Huh? We Have?

2. Contact your hotel and ask them if they have parking (rare) and if not, are you permitted to stop outside the hotel and unload your luggage?

3. Ask for the *exact name* and *exact address* of the nearest parking lot and the name of the entrance/exit closest to your hotel.

4. If you are not permitted to enter the old town by car at all, as is the case in San Sebastian — Spain, Avignon — France, Ostuni — Italy, ask your hotel for the name of the closest parking lot and the address of the entrance to the lot. San Sebastian, for example, has an underground lot that extends beneath several city blocks. You could have to walk quite a distance if you don't have this information,

and wheeling suitcases along bulging cobblestones can be pretty tedious.

5. Often cabs are allowed into old towns to pick up and drop off passengers. If that's the case, park in a lot outside the town and call a cab. It's generally the most hassle-free and best option.

6. Note: The small hotels and B&Bs sometimes have discount coupons at nearby parking lots for their guests.

7. If you plan to drive in and out of the old historical towns, try not to rent an SUV. Some of the little one-way streets are so narrow (for example — Toledo) that you only have inches to spare on either side. SUVs have become increasingly popular with European car rental companies.

How to Plan Your Wardrobe

One of the biggest headaches when traveling is luggage, especially when visiting multiple countries and combining adventure with culture and varying climates. We have found that the lighter we travel, the more pleasant the trip. However, not having the right gear can make one downright miserable, especially if shopping opportunities are scarce and you are on a budget. I hope that 'How to Plan Your Wardrobe' helps you narrow it down and lighten your load.

Check your itinerary and make notes:

1a. What is the weather likely to be in each destination — plan for that and the exact opposite. Example: We planned on hiking in Switzerland in July — it snowed. Europe can be sizzling in summer or be flooded with non-stop rain.

1b. Does any part of your itinerary call for formal wear? Example: an elegant restaurant, a symphony concert, a formal dinner party?

1c. Will you be visiting churches, temples, synagogues, mosques, wats, or other holy places? If so, for women, make sure you have a long-sleeved blouse that is not sheer or a shawl that you can wrap around your upper body to cover your shoulders and arms. Some religious establishments require both men and women to cover their heads, while it's a no-no in others.

1d. Read up on what may be considered inappropriate dress in the countries you'll be visiting. Example: Americans are very comfortable being out on the street in shorts and leggings, but in many countries, it's inappropriate and disrespectful.

1e. Do certain colors have a specific meaning in the country you'll be visiting? Example: white can signify death and mourning in one country, purity and virginity in another, and absolutely nothing in another. Red signifies love, passion, danger, and aggression in the West; in Asia: good luck, happiness, and prosperity; in Russia, it's associated with something beautiful and honorable, and in South Africa with mourning and aggression.

2. When planning your wardrobe, set your clothes out on your bed where you can see them all together. Mix and match them to create as many outfits as possible using as few clothing items as possible. Tip: pack a lightweight scarf, and a string of beads, and be creative. The goal is to try and pack as little as possible without feeling as though you look the same day in and day out. Remember: whether you plan to or not, you are highly likely to purchase odds and ends along the way.

3a. Choose a color scheme. I like dark gray as opposed to black — black shows marks, and if you happen to wear a scarf or sweater that sheds, you'll be covered in gray or white bits of fluff, which is not to say that I don't always have a couple of black items as a staple.

3b. I also like taupe and greens for travel gear. These team up with gray, black, camel, lighter shades of green, rusty tones, and oatmeal.

This color palette can be boring — especially when worn day in and day out — but it works, and traveling light adds so much to the enjoyment of one's trip.

The basics of my travel wardrobe:

4a. A couple of pairs of good-looking, fast-drying cargo/hiking pants — with lots of pockets. Preferably at least one where the legs zip off, leaving me with a pair of shorts for hot weather, cycling, working out, etcetera.

4b. A couple of short-sleeve tees — that are good quality and preferably quick-drying.

4c. A couple of long-sleeve tees that can be worn tied around my shoulders, which also saves space in the suitcase. Air conditioning in airports, stores, trains, and buses can be icy, so have something warm and light on hand.

5. Outerwear: instead of traveling with a bulky coat, I like to have layers that I can wear all together in frigid weather or individually when it's warm.

5a. I never travel without a lightweight soft fleece that can be tied around my waist to save space in my luggage and keep me warm if the weather suddenly turns when I'm out and about. I like REI, North Face, Columbia, and Patagonia brands.

5b. For cold weather, a down jacket provides excellent insulation. The latest ones are not bulky, and they're lightweight.

5c. A waterproof outer shell that I wear over my down jacket when it's cold and wet, and I always take waterproof pull-on long pants. These are available at stores like REI. You don't want to huddle indoors and miss a day of exploring because it's raining. So wrap yourself in waterproof gear, top it all off with a very lightweight plastic poncho if necessary, and a good umbrella, and you'll be snug, dry, and comfortable.

6. A pair of leggings that can be worn under my lightweight slacks in cold weather, can also be used as PJs and workout clothing. UNIQLO makes the most comfortable leggings called Heattech that are soft and thin, and keep one nice and warm.

7. If we are traveling in a cold climate, I pack a lightweight warm scarf or pashmina, gloves, and woolen cap.

8. Quick-drying underwear.

9a. A sunhat that is light and shades my face, neck, and ears. Remember that the winter sun can also be brutal. Examples: Patagonia, Tibet, Iceland, and Uyuni.

9b. A bathing suit and flip-flops. Even when visiting a cold climate, there may be hot springs, geothermal pools, spas, and indoor pools, which call for a bathing suit.

9c. If you are traveling in summer, a sarong is extremely versatile. You can wear it as a shawl when you need to cover your arms and shoulders; as a skirt with a tee-shirt; as a beach wrap; as a wrap to cover up when answering the door to room service, etcetera. Have fun experimenting with the different ways of knotting it. In many countries (especially Asia), it's common for both men and women to wear sarongs.

10a. Shoes. Good-looking, slip-on flip-flops (not thongs that fit between the toes). I pack them in my backpack so that I can remove my shoes and wear them with socks when traveling by plane or train and give my feet a rest from closed shoes. They can also be worn to the swimming pool, the beach, or out on the street.

10b. If your itinerary calls for some serious hiking and climbing in rugged terrain, or you expect to encounter rainy weather, wear lightweight, waterproof, low tops or medium top boots that have been worn in. Wear your heaviest shoes when you are traveling between destinations to avoid having to pack them. No matter what the season, if you are caught in a downpour, it's great to have waterproof shoes.

10c. A lightweight comfortable pair of shoes for the hours of walking you are most likely to be doing. I like Adidas and Hoka One One, which are sinfully ugly, but I can walk in them forever. They have great soles that cushion all those bulging cobbled stones, and they are exceptionally lightweight.

10d. For women — if you plan on dressing up a little — a lightweight pair of elegant sandals or soft shoes that take up very little space in your suitcase.

10e. I pack my shoes in thin plastic supermarket vegetable bags or disposable shoe covers, then slide them into shoe socks. If you can't find travel shoe socks, save some of the free airline socks that they give you on long flights and use those. You don't want smelly shoes among your clothes, so change the plastic bag and wash the socks frequently.

10f. To avoid any odor caused by shoes, open a couple of bars of soap and scatter them in your suitcase. Be careful that the soap has a pleasing and not overpowering scent.

11. A pair of compression socks to wear on long flights. They weigh nothing and help to prevent swelling of the feet and ankles.

12. If your itinerary and plans call for more dressy attire — a pair of black or dark gray slacks or a black skirt for women is very versatile. They can be dressed up by accessorizing with an attractive scarf or some beads and earrings.

13a. Leave all valuable jewelry at home. I wear a silver watch, a silver band on my wedding finger, and a pair of silver earrings. The only other piece of jewelry I may pack is a strand of inexpensive beads. Not only do you not want your valuables stolen, but you don't want to attract attention. Tip: avoid wearing clothing that display designer labels.

13b. Reminder: don't wear fake jewelry that looks like the real thing. Thieves can't always tell the difference, so you'll be mugged or have your hotel room burgled all for the sake of fake jewelry!

How to pack your suitcase:

14a. If you want an organized suitcase where you can separate items and lift out what you need at a glance, take a look at eBags packing cubes on ebags.com. You'll find some well-designed, lightweight packing containers.

14b. Some travelers prefer to roll up their clothing tightly, which reduces creasing and makes it easier to identify clothing; others prefer to pack everything as flat as possible, filling in the corners with small items like underwear and pressing everything down. Experiment and decide which method works best for you.

14c. On our long international trips — I pack a roll-on with the clothes that we'll need for the next three to four days before moving on to the next destination. This avoids having to unpack the suitcases, and we don't miss a beat if they go missing for several days.

15. Planning your trip to countries that all have the same climate at a particular time of the year can significantly reduce the amount of luggage that you'll need.

Items that Make Life Happier while Traveling

Thieves have been known to cut the straps of one's handbag or backpack — particularly prevalent in Vietnam and Thailand, for example.

1a. I wear a Pacsafe backpack with steel cabling in the shoulder straps and the backpack's frame. The inside RFID pockets prevent the scanning of credit cards and personal information.

1b. I pack a small Pacsafe RFID handbag, which I wear strapped across my torso for days when I don't need to carry my backpack.

2. Purchase metal hooks from REI, which attach to the loops of my slacks and my backpack. I use them to carry my camera on my waist, sunglasses in a case, a small bottle of hand sanitizer — anything that I want to have on hand.

3a. I take newly purchased cargo pants to my tailor and have him put zippers on the inside of pockets and studs under pocket flaps. On travel days, I carry the passports in my cargo pants' front pocket that have hidden zippers or hard-to-open studs. I place a small amount of cash in another front pocket. If your pockets don't have zippers or studs, use a large safety pin under the pocket's flap to protect your valuables from pickpockets.

3b. When out sightseeing, I carry as little as possible and make maximum use of front pockets and hooks attached to the front of my waistband.

4. Large amounts of cash should be carried in a money pouch that fits around your waist and is worn inside your slacks.

5a. As an extra precaution, place a thick elastic band around your wallet. It serves two purposes: pickpockets have a harder time sliding it out of your pocket; items don't accidentally fall out if the dividers stretch.

5b. Carry some supermarket vegetable-bag ties. Use them to tie the pull tabs of your backpack zipper together making it more difficult for thieves to unzip your backpack.

6. The more you carry hidden on your person, the happier you will be. If you don't have concealed, safe pockets, use items like wrist wallets, and workout gear tee-shirts with zipper pockets in the front, or the upper arm. I am not a fan of using pockets in sweatshirts, hoodies, and jackets. When you warm up or go to the bathroom, you remove them, and that's when you forget the jacket, or someone picks it up, and all your valuables go with it.

7. If you don't use a Pacsafe RFID purse — wear a dowdy, boring sling bag across your torso and rest your hand on it to let thieves know that you are on your guard.

8a.A mini flashlight — (a must).

8b. Extra batteries (they can be hard to find and expensive). Note: find out at check-in whether batteries must be transported in your carry-on bag or checked luggage.

8c. A headlamp — invaluable for remote areas where there is no electricity or when electricity fails.

9. A travel scale for weighing your luggage before you reach the airline check-in counter.

10a. Your eyeglass prescription and contact lens prescription.

10b. Throw away daily use contact lenses are the most convenient ones when traveling. *Note:* If you are doing adventure travel to remote places, you don't want to get eye infections or corneal ulcers. To avoid this, never sleep with your contact lenses in your eyes, and always use daily throw-away lenses. Make sure your hands are clean before touching the lenses.

11. A portable cell phone charger.

12. A voltage converter. The U.S. voltage is 100-120V. In many countries, it's 200–240V. If your device doesn't have dual voltage, you'll need a voltage converter. Not all devices require a voltage converter. For example, most cell phones do not; however, you'll still need an adapter.

13a. A set of travel adapters that allow a device from one country to be plugged into the electrical outlet of another country.

13b. Carry an adapter with multiple USB ports which enables you to charge multiple devices at the same time.

14. A pocketknife (in your checked luggage only).

15. A small pair of binoculars — especially if you will be in areas with interesting bird and animal life.

16. Water purifying tablets if you'll be trekking or in areas where the water could be sketchy.

17. Pack a doorstop for those times when you feel that your room could do with some extra security.

18. An emergency self-defense safety alarm can be carried on a key ring in your pocket. Don't have it on your person when going through security.

19a. I pack a small pillbox in my backpack with a couple of each of the following tablets: Imodium for diarrhea, Bonine for motion sickness, Tylenol for a headache or fever, Ibuprofen for aches and pains, Nyquil cold tablets.

19b. Carry your prescription medications in your carry-on luggage and make sure that they have the doctor's and pharmacy's names on them. Some countries can be strict about this.

19c. Place a few Band-Aids of different sizes in your backpack. It's not always easy to buy a decent Band-Aid when you need one. Pack an Ace Bandage for wrist, ankle, and foot sprains.

20. Pack a miniature-size bottle of rubbing alcohol and alcohol pads to be used for cuts and scrapes or to sterilize items such as scissors, tweezers, and surfaces on airplanes, busses, trains, etcetera.

21. Elastic bands are useful for binding items together in your luggage. Metal binder clips are handy for keeping curtains tightly closed.

How to Avoid Unexpected Travel Hassles

1a. Call your bank and credit card company before you leave home and advise them that you will be charging expenses to your card and withdrawing money in foreign countries. They'll ask which countries you will be visiting, your date of departure, and your return. Not only does this prevent them from blocking a transaction, but some card companies will send you email alerts if they think the activity on your card looks fishy.

Note: Some credit card companies do not require you to notify them, especially if you have a track record of foreign travel.

1b. If you are traveling outside the U.S.A. for over ninety days, your bank will most likely require you to call them and extend the foreign travel request to withdraw from ATMs abroad.

2. Many airline carriers offer a class between economy and business class. Economy Plus gives more legroom, carry-on allowance, priority boarding, etcetera. The upgrades vary from carrier to carrier. With some airlines, the difference in benefits are minimal; with

others, it's significant. Check whether the additional benefits the airline is offering are worth the extra cost.

3. Make sure that you confirm your flights and get boarding passes if you are taking an internal flight, especially in foreign countries. You can confirm on the internet twenty-four hours before departure. Domestic flights can be sketchy in some countries. You'll need your passport information and ticket confirmation code to check-in online.

4. Research carry-on weight allowance.

Some foreign countries' carriers are very strict and their limits very low, even though the overhead compartments are half-empty during the flight. Most annoying!

5. We always pack a travel scale and weigh our luggage before arriving at the airport to avoid unnecessary hassles.

6. When entering certain countries, passport control gives you an official stamped loose piece of paper. Example: Vietnam and Peru. Do not lose it. You'll need to show it when leaving the country and sometimes at hotels. Not being able to produce the slip of paper can cause major delays and hassles.

7. To avoid delay at customs on arrival at a foreign destination, make sure that you have the name and address of the place where you'll be staying. Some countries ask for this information, while in others, they just wave you through. Example: In India and Israel, you're likely to be

asked to produce this information while it's essential in Russia and China.

8. When rushing to get through security, avoid a line where two staff members are manning the screen. One of them could be in training, and the chances are that line will move slowly.

9. If your flight involves a lengthy stopover, you may want to spend the time having a meal, shopping, or taking a nap. A word of caution: before settling into relax mode, check the location of your departure gate. Some airports are humongous, and getting to your gate can involve taking trains, walking a great distance, and going up and down endless escalators. It's no fun to find that you've had a three to five-hour layover and you've missed your flight because you've been shopping or napping.

10. Have the address of the place where you will be staying written in the language of the country you are visiting and present this to the cab driver. Don't assume they'll speak your language.

11. Get into the habit of always carrying your hotel's business card on you in case you get lost and can't speak the language.

12a. Walk with confidence; don't tell locals that it's your first visit (you'll get taken on and ripped off); don't give more information than necessary to strangers, such as cab drivers, door attendants, hotel staff, and people you meet randomly.

12b. If you are fifty-nine-plus years old, be aware that you become perfect prey for con artists trying to take advantage of you. Do not accept unsolicited offers of help or respond to strangers who start up random conversations. Ignore them or just say: "No!" With authority.

13. Know the exchange rate in the country that you are visiting and use your phone calculator or carry a small calculator to convert to your currency. Remember, you are an easy target for being ripped off, and if you are — don't feel too bad and let it spoil your trip — you're in good company; it happens to most of us at one time or another.

14. You're on vacation, so relaxing and chilling is what it's all about. However, try to avoid the absent-minded syndrome, where you are so chilled that you become a target for pickpockets; forget to look before crossing a street; leave your stuff unattended or leave it behind on park benches, in cabs, etcetera.

15a. Make sure that your passport has sufficient blank pages. Some countries, such as South Africa, require a minimum of two blank pages.

15b. Check that your passport is valid for an additional six months from the end of the date of travel.

15c. Carry a copy of your passport at all times.

You may be required to produce it when you catch a train or a ferry. If you are driving, you may need to produce it if the police stop you. We rented a car in Slovenia with Ljubljana license plates. We were stopped in Italy and asked to produce our passports. If you make purchases within the European Union and want to claim the vat tax refund for items over 150 Euros, you'll have to produce your passport or a copy at the time of purchase. The salesperson will complete the required forms. (See the chapter 'Shopping' for the process of claiming the vat tax refund.) In several countries, museums will allow you free admission if you are over a certain age and prove your age by producing your passport. They will *not* accept your driver's license in place of a passport.

15d. Be wary of anyone posing as a police officer who randomly stops you in the street, and asks to see your passport, ID, or visa. Head straight to the nearest police station.

16. When traveling with minor children — yours or someone else's — always carry an authentic copy of their birth certificate. You may also need to produce copies of the parents' passports and signed notarized letters of permission from the parents for the child to travel with you.

17. If you register with the state department STEP plan, they'll put you in touch with local consulates/embassies, should you have an emergency.

How to Take Care of Yourself and Your Stuff

Setting out to explore the world is a magical and exciting experience. It tends to bring on what I call our la-la-land mentality: everything will be beautiful, exciting, and perfect. Ninety-nine percent of the time, it will be. But don't overlook that luggage can get lost or stolen, flights can be delayed or canceled, and one can get sick or injured. Planning ahead makes a world of difference in a difficult situation. It's like going on a cruise. You stow your life vest under your bed just in case, then immerse yourself in the pleasure of cruising.

1a. Trips involving airfare, hotels, tours, etcetera, can be costly. To protect yourself against financial loss should you get sick or suffer an injury either before or during your trip — purchase trip cancellation insurance.

1b. For trip cancellation insurance, to avoid overpaying, insure up to the amount that you have prepaid.

2. Check the dollar amount that your policy will pay for lost luggage and damaged luggage; missed connections; trip delay, trip cancellation, and interruption.

3. Make sure you read your policy, and I mean *really read it!*

3a. Read the exclusions.

3b. Read the conditions under which they will pay.

3c. Note the small print — little words and sentences — that can make a *big* difference as to whether the insurance company will pay or not. Example: having *original* receipts of purchases for your lost, stolen, or damaged items when they are over a certain dollar value. For reimbursement of additional expenses incurred by you due to trip delay, a claim for costs incurred must be accompanied by receipts and must be considered reasonable.

4. Some insurance policies include additional benefits such as losses due to identity theft, travel assistance, travel medical assistance, etcetera.

5. Medical expenses, dental expenses, and emergency evacuation insurance, can be combined with your trip cancellation and trip interruption insurance in one policy. Again, make sure you read and understand the coverage and the limitations. I would suggest that you Google reviews for several insurance companies and their travel insurance plans and pay special attention to people's reviews regarding their paid claims. Here are several sites: insuremytrip.com, aardvark.com, squaremouth.com, worldnomads.com, and travelinsurance.com will provide a comparison of different carriers.

6. Cancel For Any Reason insurance can be an excellent option. It costs roughly 40% more than average travel insurance and reimburses up to 75% or less of the cost of your trip. It also may require cancellation forty-

eight hours before departure, but these policies have greater flexibility and get you out of most of the exclusions that other travel insurance policies have.

7. MedjetAssist: in the event of a serious medical situation, MedjetAssist will airlift you on a private plane with a qualified doctor and nurses back home to the door of the hospital of your choice.

8. Pay the extra cost at the airport to get your checked luggage 'shrink' wrapped. It just makes it less appealing for thieves to choose your suitcase.

9. Take photos of the items in your suitcase.

Should you need to claim for lost or stolen items, you'll have a better chance of being paid in a timely manner by the insurance company. Arrange everything on your bed or a table and take clear photographs.

10. When traveling from one destination to another, always attach a luggage ID tag that gives the address of the place you will be staying at, an email address and a telephone number. This helps when your luggage doesn't make a flight or goes missing. It doesn't help to have a tag with only your home address if you're traveling for the next four weeks.

11. Take a photo of your bags just before you check them in at the airport. Make sure the photo shows the brand of the suitcases. If they go missing the better you can describe them, the greater the chances are of having them located and forwarded to you.

12. Look after your baggage claim ticket until you have recovered your baggage. The airline staff often

attaches your claim ticket to your boarding pass at check-in, which is easy to misplace on the airplane under your seat, on the floor, or in the seat pockets. Being able to give the airline the tracking number helps them to locate missing luggage.

13. Take a moment to check your boarding pass and make sure that all the details are correct. Check that your name is printed correctly. In Vietnam, at check-in at a local airport, they printed my husband's middle name instead of his first name. On a second occasion, we were issued two boarding passes in my husband's name. If you don't catch the error before going through security, they send you back to the check-in counter, where you'll wait in line again to go through security. If this happens, ask to speak to a supervisor. Sometimes they'll agree to escort you so that you can bypass the lines.

How to Make Your Flight more Comfortable
The ABC of it

What you eat and drink before a long flight and during the flight has a lot to do with how comfortable your journey will be and how you will feel when you arrive at your destination. While the airline controls almost everything that affects your comfort, the following are things that you can control.

A)1. Avoid alcohol, coffee, tea, and carbonated drinks. They increase dehydration.

2. Water is your best friend when flying. Drink lots of it. Consider carrying an empty, lightweight water bottle through security and filling it before you board. *Caution:* Ensure that water from the faucet is safe to drink before filling your water bottle at an airport.

3. Yes, drinking lots of water will mean that you will need to visit the bathroom often, and that's a good thing. It forces you to get up and move and can help to avoid blood clots in your legs.

4. Don't eat a big, heavy meal before boarding the airplane or during the flight. It's hard for your body to digest when you are inactive.

5. Avoid sugar, dessert, and candy. Opt instead for a banana, strawberries, an orange, freeze-dried fruit, unsalted nuts, unsalted crackers, and carrot sticks. *Caution:* Leave any uneaten fruit or vegetables on the airplane. *Do not* take it to a foreign country.

6. Consider carrying a few herbal tea bags and ask the flight attendants for a cup of hot water. Ginger and peppermint tea are good for nausea and digestion, and chamomile helps you to relax.

7. Avoid spicy food, oily food, and fried food. Avoid the bloaters: cabbage, baked beans, broccoli, lentils, brussel sprouts, raw onions, and for those who are prone to bloating, apples. Carbonated drinks also increase the build-up of gas in the stomach.

8. Do eat protein: skinless chicken, turkey, salmon, the white of hard-boiled eggs, and protein bars.

9. If you have a night flight, opt for foods high in carbohydrates: pasta, and rice, etcetera, which can help you fall asleep.

B)1. Wear comfortable, loose-fitting clothing. Focus on comfort, not style. Consider long pull-up pants cropped at the ankle so that they don't touch the lavatory floor. Bloating is common when you fly no matter what you eat, so avoid wearing clothing that is tight on the waist. Wear your heaviest shoes to save space and weight in your luggage, and pack a pair of soft slip-ons in your carry-on luggage. I always pack a pair of lightweight Crocs sandals to wear during the flight. Wear compression socks to avoid swelling of your ankles.

2. Don't forget a lightweight, warm sweater. I also knot a long-sleeved tee-shirt around my shoulders. The cabin can be freezing, and you'll save space in your checked luggage by wearing these two items. The vast majority of domestic flights no longer provide blankets, so avoid dressing as though you're going to the beach.

3. Remove your contact lenses, use hydrating eye drops, and wear your eyeglasses.

4. Moisturize your face and apply hand cream regularly.

5. As a courtesy to fellow passengers, don't wear colognes and perfumes. So many people are seriously allergic these days.

6. Always have a face mask with you and wear it if anyone is sneezing or coughing. In a confined, tight space, you are susceptible to catching whatever is going around. (Note: I have always carried masks, even pre-Covid 19. Some cities have horrific pollution, which makes breathing difficult. Mexico City, Ho Chi Minh City, and Delhi — to name a few).

C) Exercise during the flight.

There are several exercises that you can do in your seat without disturbing the person next to you and others that you can do standing in line for the bathroom or at the back of the plane when the flight attendants aren't busy with food carts.

Check your medications. Some medications (for example, hormone tablets) and some medical conditions (for example, varicose veins) may increase your risk of blood clots. Wear compression socks, drink lots of water, walk the aisle frequently, and exercise your ankles and calves.

1. Ankle circles: sitting with your left foot on the floor, circle your right foot outwards ten times, then inwards ten times. Do two to three sets, alternating the right and left foot.

2a. Feet flat on the floor, lift your toes and hold for five seconds. Do it ten times.

2b. Feet flat on the floor, lift your toes and keep heels on the floor, turn your feet out as far as you can hold for five seconds, return to the center, and relax. Do it five times.

3. Marching on the spot. Sit upright with feet flat on the floor hip-width apart. Lift right knee, hold for three seconds, and relax. Repeat in a marching motion fifteen to thirty times.

4. Hug your left knee to your chest, hold for ten seconds, and relax. Repeat with the right knee. Do three to four sets.

5. Stretch your legs under the seat in front of you. Flex at your ankles (toes up heels down), hold for five seconds, point your toes and hold for five seconds. Repeat several times.

6. Stretch your lower back. Sitting straight up in your seat, place your hands on the outside of your left thigh and turn your body to the left. Feel the stretch in your lower back and hold for ten seconds. Repeat on the right.

7. Sitting in your seat, stretch your hips by placing your left ankle on your right knee. Place your hands on your left knee and gently press down. Hold for ten seconds. Repeat on the right.

8. Roll your shoulders gently forward four times and backward four times. Do several sets standing at the back of the airplane:

9a. Lean forward from the waist and try to touch your toes. Don't force it.

9b. Place your left foot on the inside of your right knee and gently push your left knee out. Hold for five seconds. Repeat with the right foot on the inside of the left knee. Do three sets.

9c. Clasp your hands behind your back, your palms level with your butt and facing the floor, push your palms towards the floor and keep your shoulders back. Hold ten seconds and relax.

9d. Place your hands against a wall surface.
With your right knee bent and the toes of your right foot against the base of the wall, stretch your left leg out behind you, pressing your heel to the ground so that you feel a stretch in the calf of your left leg. Hold for fifteen seconds and repeat with the right leg.

9e. Bend your right arm behind your back.
Hold onto your right elbow with your left hand and pull gently to the left. Hold for ten seconds and switch arms.

How to Cope with Jet Lag

Experts agree that it takes approximately one day for each time zone crossed to adapt completely to a new time zone. Therefore, the greater the number of time zones crossed, the more severe the jet lag and the longer it takes to get over it. So be patient with your body and adopt 'jet lag recovery' behavior.

1. If you depart on a daytime flight and arrive at your destination at night, try not to sleep too much during your flight. Conversely, if you have a night flight and arrive at your destination in the middle of the day, try and have a good 'night's sleep on the plane.

1. Set your watch to your destination's local time so that you can plan ahead and sync your sleep times accordingly.

2. Avoid caffeine and alcohol, and drink lots of water. Remember that staying hydrated is key. Eat foods high in carbohydrates, not protein, before attempting to sleep. Carbohydrates help to induce drowsiness.

3. Stop using your computer an hour or more before you plan to sleep on the airplane. The light of the screen can affect your ability to fall asleep.

4. Upon arrival, get onto your destination's time zone immediately and try to avoid sleeping during the day.

5. It's important that you continue to avoid caffeine and alcohol during the adjustment period and drink water.

6. It's normal to experience headaches, nausea, and dizziness. It will pass.

7. Be active, but avoid engaging in any strenuous exercise. Get out into the daylight and fresh air, which stimulates your body to adjust. Take a walk, explore your new surroundings, browse the stores, and socialize.

8. Avoid going to bed too early. I try to stay awake until nine or ten p.m. Soak in a warm bath immediately before going to bed, and add a few drops of lavender oil or lavender salts to the water. It will help to make you sleepy. You can also put some lavender salts underneath your pillow.

9. To help you overcome jet lag, you may want to take Melatonin twenty to thirty minutes before going to sleep. Experts say that a three to five mg dose appears to be the most effective. They recommend starting with a lower dose, and if after thirty minutes, you still can't sleep, increase it slightly. Rescue sleep is an all-natural remedy, which is sprayed on the tongue just before going to sleep. It works well for some, while others find it too mild.

10. Don't be surprised if jet lag hits you a couple of days after reaching your destination.

11. If you experience more severe jet lag after some long-distance flights versus others, it's most often due to the direction of travel. The body copes more easily with flying westward — when you gain time — than eastward — when you lose time.

12. A common side effect of air travel is constipation. Eat a high-fiber diet, lots of roughage, dried fruits — especially prunes — and drink a lot of? You got it! Water!

13. *Note:* always consult your doctor before taking any remedies including natural remedies. If you feel ill after a flight it could be due to more than jet lag. Don't take chances. Consult a doctor as soon as possible.

Lost Luggage

1. Tag your bags with your home address and the address of your destination. If you plan to spend only a few days at your destination before moving on, write the farther destination's address on your tag — also your email address and mobile number and the email address of your hotel.

2. Place identifying items on your checked luggage: ribbons, colored straps, and stickers, all help to make your suitcase stand out.

3. Place your contact information on the inside of your luggage where it is clearly visible.

4. Take photos of your luggage before you reach the airline check-in counter at the airport. Make sure that your photo shows the brand name of your suitcases.

5. If your luggage does not come off the belt, check the area around the luggage carousel. Sometimes it is taken off by someone else and left standing in the general area.

6. No Luck? Head straight to the lost luggage/customer service counter, file a report, and ask the attendant at the counter to track your luggage.

7. Always look after your luggage tags handed to you when you check your luggage or printed if you do self-

check-in at a kiosk. You'll need those tag numbers to complete the lost luggage report. Ensure that you get a copy of the report, a telephone number, and an email address where you can follow up with the tracking of your luggage.

8. Once you've filled out the report, ask how you can apply for short-term reimbursement if your luggage is delayed for several days. You may need to buy a change of clothing and basic toiletries.

9. When you arrive at your hotel, ask the concierge or person at the front desk to assist you in following up relentlessly. They speak the language and most likely have dealt with lost luggage issues innumerable times.

10. You must stay on top of it. Keep calling.
Describe your suitcase in detail: brand, color, ribbons, straps, stickers. It also helps if you can describe the items you packed on top of your suitcase, in case ribbons, straps, and luggage tags have been lost en route. Sometimes it helps to go back to the airport if several days have gone by with no results. Our luggage went missing a week into our last three-and-a-half month trip. We visited the airport early in the morning and were permitted to enter the lost luggage hall with an airport representative. Much to my surprise, I found our luggage.

11. If you never see your luggage again, you can file a claim with the airline for reimbursement. Also, remember that travel insurance that you purchased before embarking on your trip? Call the insurance company and ask them how you file a claim.

12. Having experienced several lost luggage episodes, I strongly recommend that you put thought into how you pack for your trip. You don't want to waste valuable travel days consumed with missing luggage. (a) Pack all medications and any essential cosmetics in your carry-on luggage. (b) Wear extra layers on the plane: a sweater, a coat, a scarf, and your heaviest shoes. (c) Pack extra underwear and a complete set of clothing in your carry-on luggage. (d) Pack a small container of powdered clothing detergent. (e) Now you can go out and explore and not miss a beat for the next few days.

13. Half mine — half yours.
If you are traveling with a spouse, a significant other, a family member, or friend, pack half of your items in each suitcase. Just make sure that you pack complete outfits: tee-shirts, pants/shorts, bathing suit, sweater, underwear, etcetera.

Note: even if you do pack half mine — half yours, tip number twelve above is vital because often a large number of suitcases go missing.

14. Today many airlines charge for a carry-on — my advice is to pay the fee and minimize your bag's chances of going missing.

How to Stay Healthy During Your Travels

Most of us fear getting ill in a foreign country. The risk of contracting common infections can be reduced by taking precautionary steps: know which medications can be taken ahead of time to prevent getting ill in the first place, which natural remedies can help, and which self-help medications you may want to pack in your emergency kit.

1a. Wash your hands before putting anything in your mouth. Soap and water are best but not always available.

1b. When washing your hands, rub your palms together, rub the back of your hands, between your fingers, and under your nails. Wash for twenty seconds with warm water if possible, then rinse and dry thoroughly. Carry a travel-size bottle of hand sanitizer on you and a larger bottle in your suitcase to refill the miniature one.

2. Try to avoid touching your face: eyes, nose, and mouth in particular.

3. Ask the management at your hotel if it's safe to drink the water from the faucet. You can also Google it at cdc.gov/travel. Countries like Iceland, Switzerland, Belgium, Japan, New Zealand, and Sweden, for example, are safe, but *when in doubt* drink only bottled purified

water or water that has been boiled. It's not uncommon in some cities for vendors to refill water bottles and resell them to unsuspecting travelers. Make sure that you have to crack the seal to open the bottle.

4. If possible, wash or wipe down the outside of the bottle if you want to drink directly out of it. In India, my husband got infected with leptospirosis, commonly known as 'rat fever.' It could have been contracted from not washing his hands adequately before eating — or perhaps from a water bottle that a rat had run over in the store, depositing traces of urine.

5. If you plan to hike or trek in remote areas, carry water purifying tablets with you. You'll find them in camping/outdoor specialty stores such as REI.

6. Dairy products can bring on bad bouts of diarrhea and vomiting.

6a. If you find yourself in areas where milk is scarce, or refrigeration is sketchy, avoid drinking milk unless it has been boiled.

6b. My golden rule: don't eat the butter — especially in hot climates. Even reputable hotels and restaurants leave butter standing out for too long before refrigerating it, then they take it out of the refrigerator and serve it again at the next meal.

6c. Be careful with yogurt, cheese, creamy ice cream, and mayonnaise. All these can make you sick if they have been standing unrefrigerated for too long or are homemade. During our last trip, I ignored my advice. We were staying in a small boutique hotel in Aït Ben Haddou in Morocco. The breakfast consisted primarily of pancakes, bread, and jam. I was famished, so although I knew better, I ate the homemade yogurt and then suffered gastroenteritis for the next two weeks.

6d. If you are not used to a regular diet of highly spiced food, I recommend that you go easy on it. Your stomach may rebel if you overindulge.

7. Unless you are at an upscale restaurant or hotel, don't eat lettuce, tomatoes, raw corn, etcetera. It may not have been washed with purified water.

8. Eat only vegetables that have been cooked. No salads, and again, avoid mayonnaise.

9. Eat fruits that you can peel yourself unless you are eating at a reputable hotel or restaurant.

10. Eat only well-cooked food, nothing rare, especially not undercooked chicken or ground beef, and when ordering fish, make sure it's fresh.

11. Check if you will be visiting a high-altitude destination. Example: parts of South America, Tibet, Nepal, etcetera. Altitude sickness is very unpleasant and can be avoided with natural remedies (which are not always effective) or prescription medication, which we have found to be highly effective. *Note:* While taking the medication, you may get a tingling sensation in your cheeks or fingers. If this should happen, most doctors suggest that you reduce the dosage to half a tablet. Ask your prescribing doctor for his/her opinion.

12. Check if you will be visiting an area where malaria or dengue are prevalent. Medication can be taken to

prevent malaria, but not at this time to prevent dengue. The best protection against dengue is to use ointment or sprays and keep yourself covered in the early mornings and from the late afternoons onwards. I use Ultrathon insect repellent lotion. A small tube goes a long way, and it keeps these mosquitoes at bay.

Note: The above are all general guidelines that apply mostly to off-the-beaten-path and remote destinations. We have stayed in inns, homestays, and small hotels, many of which are family-run, where their standards are more trustworthy and far superior to a five-star hotel. When we hiked the Inca Trail in South America, for example, all fruits and vegetables were washed with water that had been purified and boiled. Bottom line: when in doubt, ask or abstain.

13. Remember: Always have a face mask with you and wear it if anyone is sneezing or coughing. In a confined, tight space, one is susceptible to catching whatever is going around.

14. For answers to questions regarding staying healthy in the country you will be visiting, the CDC website can be helpful. cdc.gov/travel. Select your destination, click on travel advice and resources, then scroll down until you find the item you are looking for: for example, food and drink.

Helpful Natural Remedies and Medications

1a. I don't leave home without Advil for muscular aches and pains, Tylenol or Excedrin for headaches and fevers, and Zithromax prescribed by my doctor, which is a broad-spectrum antibiotic. Get clear instructions from your physician on when it would be appropriate to use it.

1b. If you don't take a Vitamin C supplement and a probiotic on a regular basis, get into the habit of doing so religiously when you travel to give your immune system a boost.

2a. Carry Bonine for motion sickness. It does not make one drowsy and can be popped into the mouth and left to dissolve without water.

2b. Tip for lessening the effects of motion sickness: keep your eyes fixed on something in the distance like the horizon or a mountain; anything in the distance that doesn't move.

3. Pack an ankle guard or Ace Bandage that can be used for ankle, wrist, and foot sprains.

4. One of the most common ailments when traveling is a gastrointestinal infection, which can be viral or bacterial, and develops either from contaminated food or

water or through contact with someone who is infected. The symptoms are nausea, diarrhea, vomiting, and sometimes cramps and fever.

Tips to minimize the risk:

4a. Wash your hands well with soap and warm water for twenty seconds before touching anything you plan to put in your mouth.

4b. Drink only boiled or purified, bottled water.

4c. Avoid butter, mayonnaise, cream, cheese, yogurt, and creamy ice cream. Any dairy product that may not have been properly handled and refrigerated.

4d. Avoid uncooked vegetables or any fruit that you can't peel yourself.

Natural remedies that may help with nausea:

5a. A teaspoon of grated nutmeg mixed with honey helps to treat nausea and diarrhea.

5b. Chew mint leaves or steep mint leaves in boiled water for several minutes. Allow the brew to cool to a comfortable temperature and drink it. Sucking mint candy can also be helpful.

5c. Mix one teaspoon of apple cider vinegar with one teaspoon of honey, add some water, and drink. Drink three times daily with your 'meal'.

5d. I don't leave home without a prescription medication for nausea from my doctor, which I resort to if all else fails.

Note: These are all tips to help you just until you can see a competent doctor.

Natural remedies that may help a case of diarrhea:

6a. Try the nutmeg and honey remedy described in five(a) as well as the cider vinegar remedy described in five(c) above.

6b. Grate an unpeeled apple. Leave it to turn brown before eating.

6c. Adopt the BRAT diet as soon as you feel the onset of nausea and especially diarrhea: Unripe Bananas, Rice (with no oil or butter), grated Apples (grate and set aside until they turn brown), Toast (or dry crackers if toast is unavailable) and Tea (no milk).

6d. I don't set out on a trip without Imodium and prescription medication from my doctor for severe cases of diarrhea. You'll know when it's severe. I developed a bout of diarrhea on a remote island in Peru accompanied by fever, cramps, and the whole enchilada. The medication did the trick.

7. Years ago, we were given a tip by a friend of ours who is a physician from Peru — South America. He advised us to take one Pepto Bismol tablet every morning before breakfast to coat the stomach. We have followed his advice for years, and it seems to have worked pretty well.

Note: Consult your doctor. All remedies — whether natural or regular medications — can affect us differently depending on what other medications we are taking and what health issues we may have.

8. Altitude sickness can be very unpleasant and ruin a trip.

8a. Consult your doctor before leaving home.

He/she may recommend taking medication. We have taken medication on several occasions, and it has helped enormously.

8b. When you are at a high altitude: allow your body to acclimatize by walking slowly, drinking lots of water, eating lightly, and avoiding all alcohol.

8c. Natural remedies are: chewing coca leaves as they do in South America, where they are readily available, and drinking coca tea. These remedies are most likely not available in other countries. In fact, they're most likely outlawed.

9. Don't leave home without a small nasal spray for colds and allergies. When your nose is running or so blocked from a cold that you can't breathe, it'll be your best friend, and it takes up no space in your luggage.

10. A small tube (travel size) of athlete's foot ointment.

11. A small tube of Polysporin® first aid antibiotic ointment to prevent infection in minor cuts and burns.

12. Make sure that you pack your prescription medications in your carry-on luggage in case your checked luggage goes missing.

13. All prescription medication should have the doctor and pharmacy's name and telephone number on the package.

14. Get the generic name for your medications. Pharmacists in foreign countries may only know medications by their generic names.

15. Carry your eyeglass and contact lens prescriptions with you. If you wear daily contact lenses, keep the tab that you peel off in your wallet.

16. If you are a contact lens wearer, always take a pair of eyeglasses with you to wear during long flights and in case you get an eye infection.

What to do if You Need a Doctor or Hospital

1. Most of us neglect to complete the information page on the inside of our passports. Make sure it's filled out with the name and telephone number of someone to contact in the event of an emergency or an accident.

2. In the case of a severe illness, contact the embassy or consulate of your home country for a list of healthcare providers and hospitals/clinics.

3. While embassies and consulates can be most helpful, you can't always reach them when you need a doctor or hospital. So I share our personal experiences with you for what they are worth; however, I am by no means an authority on the subject. In India, Stan developed leptospirosis. It's a pretty serious condition. I asked the owners of our boutique hotel on a coffee plantation in the Wayanad Forest for assistance. They were remarkable! Within an hour, their personal physician had ordered the paramedics to come to the plantation and take a blood sample. By the next day, we had the diagnosis from a hematologist and their physician, and the appropriate medication had been prescribed. When we moved on to Fort Kochi in Kerala, the owner of that hotel provided a

driver who took us to the international private hospital where Stan went every day for a week to be monitored.

Locals, the concierge, owner/manager of your hotel, are often the fastest and most reliable resources. If possible, always choose a private or international hospital.

On a flight from the USA to Venice — Italy, Stan got ill. By the time we reached our small, family-owned hotel on the Venice canals, he had a high fever. I approached one of the owners, and within ten minutes, a water taxi ambulance arrived. They had Stan in the emergency room fifteen minutes later. The doctors and nurses were superb.

4. One should never leave one's home country without a medical, travel insurance plan and MedjetAssist coverage for emergency evacuation. (See the chapter: 'How to Take Care of Yourself and Your Stuff').

5. Be aware that there are some countries where *all* medical facilities are substandard. For example, in Myanmar, you don't want to go into one of their ill-equipped, dilapidated, antiquated hospitals. This also applies to parts of Africa, Central America, etcetera. In this case, MedjetAssist is invaluable unless you can get to a neighboring country with superior medical care.

6. For American senior citizens, be aware that Medicare will not cover you outside the U.S.A.

7. If you have a pre-existing condition, it's wise to carry a letter from your doctor describing your condition. Carry it with you. You never know when you may need it. If you are allergic to any medications, carry a list of them and a list of all prescription medications you are taking.

8. Above all — try to stay calm and think rationally unless you have a companion or spouse who can do that for you.

9. A brief word of caution: in Western societies, we are accustomed to Googling everything. While that is a great resource, a trained physician's knowledge and ability are highly respected in many countries. So be tactful if you choose to share your Google knowledge. It may be considered offensive.

Mosquitoes — Malaria, Dengue, West Nile Virus, and Zika

Before leaving home, find out if you'll be visiting a malaria area. Malaria comes from a mosquito bite, as does dengue, the Zika Virus, and West Nile Virus.

1. The best protection against mosquitoes is to be vigilant against being bitten in the first place.

2. Avoid being outdoors in a mosquito area at dawn and dusk when the winds are calm — and mosquitoes are out, hungry to feed on your juicy flesh.

3a. Mosquitoes are known to be drawn to CO_2 (carbon dioxide) and heat, so when you are outdoors at dawn or dusk working out, sweating and breathing heavily, you become their best friend.

3b. Mosquitoes are common around stagnant water. Avoid pools of stagnant water.

4a. Dressing in long sleeves, and light-colored clothing, and exposing as little skin as possible helps enormously.

4b. In areas where mosquitoes are prevalent, e.g. the Pantanal in Brazil, the Amazon Jungle, etcetera, I wear the bottoms of my slacks tucked into long socks, wear a scarf around my neck that has been pretreated with mosquito repellant (available in sporting goods and camping stores) and use a mosquito repellent ointment such as Ultrathon — (just a few drops) around my wrists. If one's arms or legs are uncovered, rub a light coating of Ultrathon on the exposed skin.

5a. If we know that we will be visiting a malarial area, we take prescription medication before arriving at our destination. *Note:* one must consult with a doctor to obtain malarial medication. We have found Malarone, which is a combination of two drugs — Atovaquone and Proguanil — to be effective and have experienced none of the horrible side effects of the malaria medication of bygone years.

5b. Important: as far as I know, there are currently no medications available to protect one against Dengue, Zika, and the West Nile Virus. So the best remedy is to protect against getting bitten in the first place.

6. When visiting areas known to be populated by mosquitoes, we soak our clothing in Permethrin — available at REI and camping goods stores. The treatment lasts for six washes. We prefer the soaking solution to the spray as it provides more thorough coverage. The first time we used Permethrin, I was concerned that the process might damage the fabric or the colors; however, we have never found this to be the case. For the best results, follow the exact directions on the container.

7. I always carry a few mosquito wipes, which come in a pack of individual sachets. I purchase them from stores like REI. One never knows when you'll find yourself out

at dusk without protective clothing — so having mosquito wipes handy is a good idea.

Here are several natural remedies that some people swear by to keep mosquitoes away.

8a. Neem oil mixed with some coconut oil, mix and rub into the skin.

8b. Catnip oil.

8c. Raw garlic or garlic oil rubbed on your skin. (You may succeed in keeping more than mosquitoes away).

9. Keeping fans going in a room and overhead outdoor fans going in the garden.

10. If one does get bitten — it can be extremely challenging to avoid scratching. Use all your willpower to avoid scratching.

11a. I always carry a tube of chamomile lotion for bites or itchy skin, also a small tube of aloe vera. Aveeno® makes an excellent anti-itch chamomile lotion.

11b. Tea tree oil is also a soothing remedy — as is rubbing a used tea bag over the itchy bites.

11c. Soaking in a bathtub of warm water to which you have added several cups of cider vinegar, also tames and calms the itch.

How to do Your own Laundry

1. Hotel laundry services may be costly.

Laundromats and cleaners are sometimes difficult to locate, and it's not uncommon for your laundry to be returned shrunken, stretched, misshapen, or nicely packaged and still damp.

2. To pack less, keep our clothing fresh, and the laundering process quick and simple, we've developed a system of doing our laundry almost daily.

2a. I pack a small Tupperware of laundry powder. Powder vs. liquid for several reasons: it goes a long way, it does not spill, and is allowed in your carry-on luggage. Most underdeveloped countries use powder, and small packets are readily available in their markets should you need to replenish them.

2b. I pack several pairs of thin surgical gloves to use when doing laundry. Without them, my hands get very dry, and the skin cracks. I don't want open cuts on my hands, which can lead to an infection. *Tip:* You may want to carry a plug for the bathroom sink just in case the plug doesn't work too well.

3. We ask the hotel for two additional large towels, extra hangers, and a hairdryer if the bathroom doesn't have one.

4. We check out the bathroom and bedroom for places to hang laundry. Here you can get creative. Example: bathroom rails, doorknobs, towel racks, handles on windows, standing coat racks, the clothes valet, etcetera.

5. We identify the driest and warmest areas to hang our laundry. Example: a heated bathroom with warm towel racks or a window where sunshine floods the room.

6. When we are in one place for two or more nights — it gives us a reasonable amount of time for the thicker clothing to dry. Everything can be washed in the bathroom sink. For some items, Stan may use the bathtub, but it's hard on the back.

7. Set to go! Fill the sink with water — add powder — not too much. The powdered stuff is concentrated and goes a long way. Wash and rinse the garments and squeeze out as much water as you can.

8. Lay a bath towel on the clean bathroom floor — you can also use the clean towel bathmat to wrap the clothes — lay several items on the towel and roll it up.

8a. Stomp (with clean feet) on the towel. Flip it over and stomp again to get rid of as much moisture as possible.

9. Hang the clothing up to dry on hangers.
Using hangers lets the air circulate and clothes dry more quickly. If available, use hangers with clips for socks, underwear, and slacks.

10. Hook the hangers on the shower curtain rod, or a towel rail, and use the hairdryer to speed up the drying process. *Make sure there is no water around and always wear rubber-soled shoes to be safe.*

10a. Don't run the hairdryer for too long, or you will burn it out.

10b. Do the drying part several times over the next two days, for a few minutes at a time.

10c. We take care to get all the water out during the stomping phase so that no water drips on the floors or carpets, and never put wet items on furniture.

11. Stain remover — I carry a small amount of liquid dish soap in a travel-size plastic bottle. Place a few drops in a small bowl or glass. Add two to three ice cubes and some cold water. Stir it up so that it bubbles. Take the corner of a dry clean white towel and soak up some of the mixtures. Dab (don't rub) the stain. Keep dabbing until the stain disappears. I use this remedy on all stains and it works ninety percent of the time.

Valuable Tips Collected Over the Years

1. When delayed at airports or enduring never-ending flights, train, bus, or car rides — one gets hungry, and very often there is nowhere to buy something to eat, or if there is, it's something your stomach will not tolerate. I always travel with small packets of trail mix (nuts and dried fruit) and protein bars. If we take a long trip — especially to remote places — I line the bottom of my suitcase with these snacks and transfer them to my daypack as needed. I also purchase small packets of plain crackers, which are generally available even in remote areas.

2. If you are a reader, I recommend that you carry an electronic device with the books you have downloaded. It saves weight and space, and most important — you won't run out of good reading material.

3. Establish a routine of keeping your stuff in the same place when you travel. It saves so much time and aggravation if you know where to find things, your glasses, iPhone, camera, the key to your room, passport, and wallet. I try to always pack items in the same part of my suitcase so that they are easy to find. Example: socks — I pack in the corners of my suitcase; hat — on the inside

flap; shoes — around the edges; toothbrush and toothpaste — against the front frame of my carry-on bag; reading glasses in the outside pocket of my backpack, etcetera.

4a. Get into the habit of checking your space *every* time you leave a spot: a coffee shop, a seat in the waiting area of an airport, a hotel room, or a tour bus. Do a quick scan of your space and the floor and chairs around it, to make sure that you leave nothing behind. It's well worth the few seconds that it takes.

4b. When leaving your hotel to move on to your next destination, don't forget to clear your room's safe. Place one of the shoes that you intend to wear in the safe.

That will definitely remind you to clear it. Always run your hand across the interior of the safe, especially the back and the corners.

5. Be careful of hanging things on the inside door and shelves of toilet stalls. Check your space before leaving, also make sure that no one can reach under or over the stall door, and steal items while you are otherwise engaged.

6. Keep your backpack safe while sitting in a restaurant, airport, etcetera. Hook your foot into the straps. Never hang it off the back of your chair unless the chair is up against a wall.

7. Need a good guide or driver? Most of our outstanding guides and drivers have come from us asking the hotel manager to find us the right person — in India, Cambodia, Peru, Vietnam, Thailand, Bali, Ecuador, and Morocco, just to name a few. We also land up seeing

places and meeting people whom we would never have had the pleasure of otherwise meeting.

8. I always email a few days ahead to confirm the time, date, and place where a driver or tour guide will be meeting us. I recommend doing this no matter which guide or tour company you use.

9a. Check the *details* of your itinerary carefully. Example: a city may have several airports that are often miles and hours apart; airport codes can be similar. In Ecuador, the tour company that had arranged our boat tour of the Galápagos Islands flew us to the wrong airport on the wrong island. What followed was an unforgettable adventure that was quite hair-raising at times.

9b. Find out what is included in your tour and what is provided by the tour company. Example: on a Galápagos boat tour, do they provide you with wetsuits, fins, and swim masks? Can they guarantee a wetsuit to fit you, e.g. an extra-small or extra-large size? Hiking the Inca Trail — do they provide the duffel bag for your clothing that the porters carry?

9c. Ask what kind of bag you should bring when hiking, trekking, riding, or taking a trip on a small boat, such as a week on the Amazon River.

10. When checking in to your hotel, don't be shy to ask to see several rooms. If you arrive late, ask if you can get an upgrade. If better accommodation is available, they may give it to you at no additional cost.

11.Wi-Fi. When you arrive at your hotel, get the Wi-Fi code from the front desk and make sure that you use *only that code* and not a similar one. Example: If the code you are given is 'Downtown Hotel Flower', don't log on to something similar such as 'Downtown Hotel Flower Lobby.' Hackers may have set up the latter code. Don't stay logged in to the hotel Wi-Fi. Log in and log out each time that you use it. Shut off the 'auto-join' on your Wi-Fi to avoid exposing your phone to hackers.

12a. Tipping: research online, and ask the hotel manager, your tour company, or locals what the tipping etiquette is in the area you are visiting. It varies significantly from one country to another as well as from one region within a country to another. In less developed areas, it may even be inappropriate to tip. In some countries — such as Japan — it is considered part of one's job to give good service. Tips are most often declined and cause embarrassment.

12b. Tipping in hotels: excluding those countries where tipping is frowned upon, I have taken to leaving a small daily tip with a note (if I know some of the languages) thanking the maid for keeping our room clean and neat. This way, I get outstanding daily service, and the staff knows that I recognize and appreciate their effort. If breakfast is included, I tip every morning.

13. Our guides and drivers give so much of themselves and rely on tips to make a decent living. Yet, it's astonishing how often visitors will say, "Thank you" and walk off without tipping. Consider factoring in the cost of tipping guides and drivers when planning your itinerary so that you have budgeted for tips. 10% — 20%

depending on the country's tipping customs, and whether it's a large group tour, a small group tour, or a private tour.

14. The minibar in your hotel room: the price of items stocked in the minibar is exorbitant. Be aware that some minibars have sensors that charge you anytime you put your hand in and take something out of the unit. I was stashing a small carton of milk and my chocolate in a minibar but never removed any of the items provided by the hotel. On check out, I was presented with a hefty bill. The hotel removed the charges, and we had a good laugh about my expensive nightcap of milk and chocolate. You may want to ask the hotel to empty the minibar so that you can stock it with the drinks and snacks to your liking.

15. Ask the hotel staff for their recommendations of interesting places and neighborhoods to explore and their favorite restaurants, cafés, and bars. You'll discover some gems that you would never find in a guidebook, TripAdvisor, or city guide.

16. If you choose to eat or drink on main piazzas and plazas because you'd like to immerse yourself in the great vibe and energy they exude, expect the food to generally be inferior and the prices to be superior. You're paying for the location and ambiance. Check out the lesser piazzas and side streets where the locals gather. You'll most likely come across atmospheric places and superior dining at more favorable prices.

17. B&Bs, Airbnbs, Apartment rentals, and small hotels can have steep, winding, narrow steps, no elevator, and no one to assist you in getting your luggage up to your

accommodation. Remember to inquire when you make your reservation whether your accommodation is on the ground or upper floors and if it is the latter, do they have an elevator. If you have heavy luggage, you may not want to be dragging it up and down steps.

18. When visiting a popular destination such as the Vatican, the Alhambra, the Eiffel Tower, the Colosseum, or the Hermitage Museum, etcetera, purchase your tickets online in advance to avoid long lines.

19. Get an early start:

Visiting popular sites can be disappointing when they are overrun by tour groups. Arrive early in the morning, just before the site opens, and you'll have the place virtually to yourself until mid-morning. We watched the early morning mist rise like a bridal veil to reveal the splendor of the Taj Mahal; felt what it must have been like to discover the rock-hewn temples and monasteries of Ellora and Ajanta with no one but the langur monkeys present; encountered a mere handful of locals when we walked the walls of Old Town Dubrovnik where red-roofed stone houses glow in the morning light; had unobstructed views of the Army of Terra Cotta Warriors in Xian; hiked the Jinshanling section of the Great Wall of China and had it all to ourselves for the first two hours of our hike; visited the Colosseum in Rome (buy tickets online in advance) in high season, and wandered through it picturing the gladiators, the chariots, and cheering crowds, before umbrella-toting guides and their charges flooded in; chugged along Tonlé Sap Lake in Cambodia when the villagers who live in the water were preparing breakfast and ferrying children to the school that stands on stilts in the lake.

Tip: Angkor Wat — visitors pack into the main sanctuary to watch the sunrise over Angkor. It's chaotic! Arrive at 7.45 a.m. when the early-morning wave of visitors flows out and returns to the hotels for breakfast. You'll be treated to the tranquility and mystical aura of Angkor blanketed in silence and caressed with sunshine.

The ruins of Pompeii — if you can't get there early in the morning, go at around four p.m. when the tours are boarding their buses. The back entrance closes late. Discovering Pompeii with no one but the groundskeepers present takes the experience to another level.

Museums are often best visited towards the end of the day when there is only a trickle of visitors. Check online for the most popular times and avoid those hours if possible.

20a. If you can converse a little in the local language, it can make a world of difference. Not only is it helpful to you, but it allows you to interact with the people, which adds a whole other dimension to the enjoyment of your travels. Even if you butcher the languages, locals are touched by your efforts.

20b. Google Translate is a great help and essential in remote parts of the world where locals are unlikely to speak English or the Romance languages.

Preparing Your Home For Your Absence

1. Switch off the water at the main valve. If a pipe bursts while you are gone, it could flood your home and do severe damage.

2. Disconnect the water dispenser in your refrigerator. You may need to call in your plumber to show you how or Google it. If it malfunctions, it will flood your kitchen.

3. Give a neighbor and family member the keys to your home and a copy of your itinerary.

4. Have a neighbor park in your carport/driveway if that's where you usually park. That way, it appears that someone is staying in your home.

5. Either have someone collect your mail daily or if you are gone for a significant period of time, contact your local post office (this is done online in most cities in the U.S.A.) and request that they stop delivery from your date of departure until you return.

6. Leave music playing in your home. You can set it to go on and off with a timer.

7. Have a friend or neighbor check your home weekly. It's good for passersby to see people coming and going.

8. If you receive a daily or weekly newspaper, ask a neighbor to collect it or stop delivery.

9. If you have an alarm, make sure that you give the names and telephone numbers of neighbors or family members who should be called if the alarm goes off. Make sure that these contacts know the alarm code.

10. Use a timer to have several lights come on inside your home in the evening and switch off at whatever would be your usual 'lights-out' time.

Etiquette

Read up on the customs of your chosen destination to avoid inadvertently insulting anyone.

1. Clothing. While Westerners are accustomed to wearing shorts, tight leggings, and exposing their midriffs and shoulders in public, this style of dress is inappropriate in many Asian, African, and Middle Eastern countries.

2a. When visiting religious or spiritual places in Asia, the Middle East, and parts of Africa, shoes and socks should always be removed before entering.

2b. Women must cover their arms, shoulders, and legs. Men should not wear shorts or tank tops. They should dress conservatively.

3a. Throughout Southeast Asia the head is considered to be the most spiritual and sacred part of the body, therefore, one should never touch the head of a child or an adult.

3b. The feet are considered to be the lowliest part of the body. Never put your feet on a chair or table. When sitting on the floor make sure that the soles of your feet do not point towards anyone and especially not toward statues of Buddha or monks engaged in prayer and meditation.

3c. Don't sit at a level higher than your host when visiting their home.

4. *Greeting* — while shaking hands is common in the U.S.A, in many cultures, it's inappropriate to touch a member of the opposite sex in public.

India — Namaste. Place your palms together in front of your chest and bow slightly.

Cambodia, Thailand, Laos — place the palms of your hands together in front of you but not touching your chest, and dip your head in a slight bow.

Japan — a small nod of the head or bow is informal. A deep bow indicates respect.

China — if you are on formal terms bow slightly or nod. A handshake is appropriate for a casual greeting. Always greet older people first and if you are seated, stand up when being introduced.

Russia — a handshake if it's a formal greeting between men, and a simple nod of the head if it's a man to woman. A kiss on both cheeks is common between friends.

Mexico, Costa Rica, Columbia, Chile, Peru — an air kiss on the right cheek. In Peru, it's an air kiss on the right cheek or a handshake.

Argentina — a handshake and nod of the head while maintaining eye contact. 'Abrazo' is an informal Argentinian greeting. You shake hands and at the same time lightly graze both cheeks.

Morocco — a handshake and/or two kisses on the left cheek then the right. No touching between men and women in public.

5. *Eating* — in India, parts of the Middle East, and South East Asia, the left hand is used for toileting and dirty tasks. Only the right hand should be used for eating, serving, handshaking, giving a tip, etcetera.

6a. *Hand signs and body language* — my best advice is to Google them country by country so that an innocent gesture doesn't land you in trouble.

6b. The following are some examples of hand signs and body language that could get you into trouble. Thumbs up is interpreted as giving the middle finger in the Middle East and Africa, as is the V sign. The OK sign — making a circle with the thumb and index finger is also interpreted as giving the middle finger in several countries. Raising the index and pinky finger is considered obscene in many European countries. Crossing your fingers in Vietnam refers to the female genitals and is very rude. In Germany and Sweden, it's a sign of lying. Avoid pointing with your index finger. It's considered rude in most countries. In Cambodia, Japan, Indonesia, Malaysia, and China it's a no-no.

6c. While in the West and many other countries, shaking your head from side-to-side means 'no', in Greece, Turkey, Egypt, Iran, Lebanon, and Bulgaria. It means 'yes'.

*The head bobble in India signifies agreement or understanding.

*In Japan, nodding during a conversation conveys that you are listening. It's a gesture of politeness and does not necessarily mean agreement.

6d. Standing close to someone while talking is customary in some countries: Argentina; Peru and Bulgaria for example. While maintaining a distance is expected in Romania, Saudi Arabia, and Hungary.

6e. Winking — can be interpreted as flirting, friendly agreement, or having sexual connotations. The Chinese consider it offensive.

7. Punctuality:

*In Greece being thirty to forty minutes late is expected.

*In Mexico it's OK to be late thirty minutes to one hour.

*In Morocco several hours or even a day late are acceptable.

*In China up to ten to twelve minutes is acceptable.

*In Saudi Arabia — thirty minutes to an hour is acceptable.

*In Brazil it is customary to be late.

*Russians generally place little importance on punctuality.

*In Germany, England, Japan, Korea, and the U.S.A — it's expected and considered to be rude, unreliable, and selfish, to be late.

8. The meaning of colors:

Being aware of the meaning of colors in different cultures can avoid embarrassing situations.

Red: in most Western cultures signifies danger, anger, love, and passion. In China, it symbolizes fire, good, luck, happiness, and prosperity, and is worn to celebrate the

Chinese New Year. In Russia, red symbolizes love, courage, fire, generosity, and a young woman ready for childbearing.

Black: is often associated with mourning, death, and bad luck. In China, it represents evil and sadness, while in Russia it is associated with old age.

White: in the West, white symbolizes peace, purity, and elegance. Hence the popularity of the white wedding gown. In Asian countries, it represents the opposite: death, mourning, and bad luck. In Russia, it signifies nobility and honesty.

Yellow: in many parts of the world yellow is associated with sunshine and spring flowers. It signifies warmth and happiness. Yet in France and Germany, it often signifies jealousy and betrayal. In most parts of the Middle East, yellow symbolizes joy, however, in Egypt, it is a sign of mourning. In China, yellow is associated with good luck, prosperity, and power, but also with pornography.

Blue: in many countries, blue represents the sky and the sea and therefore is a color of peace and spirituality. In Russia, it is linked to honesty and faithfulness. In some cultures, it is thought to ward off evil. In central and South America, it is generally associated with mourning.

Green: in China, green is hope, harmony, and springtime, which brings new opportunities. In the Middle East, green is the color of tranquility, balance, and respect, whereas in Western countries it's often linked to envy, inexperience, and greed. As the common saying goes: 'To be green with envy'.

9. Avoid controversial topics and political discussions. Don't make judgmental or critical comments. Keep your jokes to yourself. You never know how they may be misinterpreted.

10. Don't take photos of members of the military, police, protests, etcetera.

11. If you are invited into the homes of locals, research the etiquette. For example, in Morocco, the woman will prepare the food but will not eat it with her guests.

12. In the U.S.A most public swimming pools post signs requesting that swimmers shower before entering the pool. Many swimmers ignore the request. In some countries, Japan and Iceland for example, it's strictly enforced. Showering removes lotions, sweat, fecal matter, etcetera and helps to avoid recreational water infections.

Shopping Tips

1. Read up on the customs of the countries that you will be visiting. In some countries, bargaining is a way of life. While in most Western countries, it's not appropriate, which doesn't mean that a polite negotiation never pays off.

2. If you shop for gifts and trinkets in busy tourist areas, you will pay more. If your tour guide takes you to a store, you are more than likely going to pay more, as the store is paying the guide to lead you there. This also applies to taxis, tuk-tuks, etcetera, in many Asian countries.

3. If you are shopping for antiques, carpets, jewelry, woodwork, and genuine handmade items, do your homework, and if possible, get recommendations from a reliable source. Remember that the person you are buying from is an expert at passing off a factory-made object as an antique or 'Made in China' piece, as handmade ceramics, carpets, glass, etcetera.

4. Should you decide to have a store ship large items such as furniture to your home country, make sure: (a) that you are allowed to bring the items into the country and (b) that you have documentation that clearly stipulates

whether it's an antique or not and if it's wood, exactly what type of wood it is. If you don't have all the required information, it could be held by the port customs authority, and they charge steeply for every day that it's kept in their storage.

5. When shopping within the European union, carry your passport or a copy of your passport with you. As of the time of writing this, if the cost of your purchase is 150 Euros or more, you are entitled to a vat tax refund at the airport before departing the European union. However, several steps need to be followed, and storekeepers don't tell you the whole story. They know what they have to give you but have only a vague idea of how the process works in practice. To complicate matters further, you'll get different information from the tax refund offices from country to country. Can you imagine an Italian, Frenchman, German, and Spaniard all agreeing on something? Here are some steps we took, and after much back and forth, we did succeed in getting the refunds at Madrid airport.

A. The store has to complete the tax refund form, which they all have. They *must see* your passport or a photocopy. They fill out the form, sign it, attach the receipt/credit card slip, place the form in an official tax refund envelope, and give it to you.

B. At the airport of departure from the European union, your first step is to go to the vat tax office and show them the items you purchased. So *remember to pack the items in your carry-on luggage.* Have the vat tax office sign and stamp the forms.

C. You then proceed to the vat tax refund office with all your stamped paperwork to get the refund.

If you have purchased several high price items, it can be worth the effort. If it's just a couple of items, it depends on how much time you have at your airport of departure from the European union.

6. Insider merchandise pricing information from a local storekeeper. A charming story that always makes me smile:

During our first six-week visit to India, we drove many miles with our terrific drivers across the country and fell in love with the chaos, the contrasts, the customs, the color, the lush, humid south, the food, and the warmth of the people.

In Jodhpur — Rajasthan, we were lured into a store where the fabrics were particularly gorgeous by the owner's magnetic personality. This, despite our emphatic declarations that we had no desire to make any purchases. He led us down a flight of stairs to a showroom, where he and his assistant proceeded to show us some stunning fabrics. Seeing that we were holding steadfast to our decision not to buy anything, he had his helper fold up all the merchandise that lay scattered around the room and served us cups of hot, sweet, chai. What followed was a congenial, humorous, and enlightening conversation. We were given the inside scoop on the rationale for the three most frequently asked questions by Rajasthani storekeepers.

Where are you from?

—If your answer is the U.S.A: they'll tell you that Bill Clinton, Richard Gere, or Lady Gaga shopped here.

—From France: it's Kathryn Deneuve or Gerard Depardieu.

—From England: David Beckham, Posh Spice, and members of the royal family.

Where are you staying?

—The Oberoi, Taj Hotels, etcetera, means the price quoted is way up there.

—A hostel or modest hotel: they show their cheapest merchandise and negotiate for the highest price that they can get.

—A medium-priced hotel: they start with high-quality merchandise and high prices and work their way down.

How long are you in India?

—If it's a long time, they are warier of ripping you off because there's more chance of you finding out you've been taken and returning to confront them.

We must have been asked these carefully thought-out questions a hundred times. It was a constant refrain.

So when shopping during your travels, enjoy the process and the interaction with the people and know that whether you get the best price or not, you're likely to have some memorable experiences.

Packing Checklist

Documents

- ◯ Passport and Copies
- ◯ Visas
- ◯ Driver's license
- ◯ Credit cards — two of them
- ◯ Cash
- ◯ ATM cards — two of them
- ◯ Airline, boat, and train tickets
- ◯ Itinerary — paper plus online copy
- ◯ Prescriptions e.g. contact lenses, eye glasses
- ◯ List of medications
- ◯ Medical insurance card
- ◯ Travel insurance card
- ◯ Medical history
- ◯ Emergency contacts
- ◯ Maps
- ◯ Hotel and tour reservation confirmations
- ◯ Copies of credit cards
- ◯ Credit card contact telephone numbers

Medications

- ◯ An adequate supply of daily medications
- ◯ Sleep aid

- ○ Motion sickness medication
- ○ Tylenol
- ○ Advil
- ○ Diarrhea medication
- ○ Nausea medication
- ○ Rubbing alcohol
- ○ Band-Aids
- ○ Ankle and foot brace
- ○ Hand sanitizer
- ○ Cold medication
- ○ Cough drops
- ○ Polysporin or Neosporin (topical antibiotic ointment)
- ○ Altitude prescription tablets for extreme altitudes

Electronics
- ○ Cell phone and charger
- ○ Camera and charger
- ○ Kindle and charger
- ○ Laptop and charger
- ○ Earphones

Clothing
- ○ Underwear panties/underpants/bras
- ○ Socks
- ○ Long pants
- ○ Shorts
- ○ Short sleeve Tee-shirts
- ○ Warm sweatshirt
- ○ Jacket
- ○ Scarf
- ○ Gloves

○ Sun hat
○ Woolen cap
○ Bathing suit
○ Beachwear cover
○ Rain jacket
○ Rain pants
○ Rain poncho
○ Exercise clothing
○ Sleepwear
○ Day bag

Formal Wear

○ Dress/skirt
○ Elegant blouse
○ Long sleeve shirt
○ Tie
○ Jacket
○ Formal slacks
○ Pantyhose
○ Belt
○ Non-valuable jewelry
○ Handbag/purse

Shoes

○ Sandals
○ Walking shoes
○ Hiking shoes
○ Formal shoes
○ Flip-flops
○ Reef shoes

Daily Basics
○ Eye glasses plus prescription
○ Reading glasses
○ Contact lenses plus prescription
○ Saline solution
○ Sunglasses
○ Suntan lotion
○ Toothbrush and toothpaste
○ Toothpicks and floss
○ Hand lotion
○ Deodorant
○ Small dual voltage hairdryer
○ Voltage converter
○ Plugs for foreign country
○ Umbrella
○ Hand mirror
○ Lip balm
○ Shampoo and conditioner
○ Soap
○ Shaving cream
○ Razor
○ Tissues
○ Female hygiene products
○ Tweezer
○ Cotton wool pads
○ Several face masks
○ Cosmetics
○ Make-up
○ Sanitary hand wipes

○ Sanitizing wipes
  (Place several in a plastic Ziploc bag and seal well)
○ Mosquito repellant
○ Comb and hairbrush
○ Nail scissors
○ Nail polish remover
○ Nail file
○ Nail polish
○ Daily vitamins
○ Small sewing kit
○ Clothes steamer
○ Clothes soap
○ Backpack

Miscellaneous

○ House keys
○ Binoculars
○ Money belt
○ Elastic bands
○ Plastic bags
○ Pens/pencils/paper/notebook
○ Plastic knife/fork/spoon
○ Sharp knife for peeling and slicing, (place in checked
  luggage).
○ Flashlight
○ Headlamp
○ Batteries
○ Luggage tags
○ Luggage locks and keys
○ Luggage straps

For plane/train

- ◯ Earplugs
- ◯ Sleep eye mask
- ◯ Reading material
- ◯ Hard candy or chewing gum
- ◯ Soft, warm socks
- ◯ Small inflatable pillow
- ◯ Slippers or flip-flops
- ◯ Snacks
- ◯ Bottled water
- ◯ Motion sickness tablets
- ◯ Sleep aid
- ◯ Face mask
- ◯ Hand sanitizer
- ◯ Sanitizing wipes for drop-down table, TV, and all controls.
- ◯ Warm sweater

Weight, Distance, Temperature, and Liquids

One ounce = 28.34 grams
One pound = 0.454 kilograms
2.204 pounds = one kilogram
One inch = 2.54 centimeters
One foot = 30.48 centimeters
One yard = 91.44 centimeters
One mile = 1.609 kilometers
Celsius — Fahrenheit
0+/-30
10+/-50
15+/-60
20+/-70
25+/-80
30+/-90
35+/-100
40+/-110
Liquids
1. U.S. gallons to liters — multiply by 3.8
2. Liters to U. S. gallons — multiply by .26
3. U. S. gallons to imperial gallons — multiply by .83

4. Imperial gallons to U. S. gallons — multiply by 1.20

5. Imperial gallons to liters — multiply by 4.55

6. Liters to imperial gallons — multiply by .22

Notes